THE
TREE

WONDER OF THE NATURAL WORLD

THE
TREE

WONDER OF THE NATURAL WORLD

Jenny Linford

BARNES & NOBLE

NEW YORK

Produced by Atlantic Publishing.

ISBN — 13: 978-0-7607-8534-8
ISBN — 10: 0-7607-8534-1

Printed and bound in China.

3 5 7 9 10 8 6 4 2

CONTENTS

INTRODUCTION

Our world without trees is impossible to imagine. Trees are the earth's oldest and largest living things. They are our planet's most complex and successful plants and have existed on Earth for 370 million years. Although there are over 80,000 different species, and despite the astonishing diversity which trees display, there is a fundamental, underlying botany which unites them. A tree is typically characterized as a self-supporting, perennial plant, capable of reaching 6m (21ft) in height, which has a single woody stem (commonly known as a trunk), roots and branches which grow from year to year.

Ever since they first appeared on the planet, trees have played an invaluable part in regulating our climate, absorbing carbon dioxide from the atmosphere and returning oxygen. For centuries mankind has turned to trees to satisfy his physical needs for fuel, for timber for housing, furniture, and tools, for medicine, and for food. They have also called out to something deeper in the soul of man, answering a spiritual need. Trees have been revered for thousands of years and feature in many of the world's great religions as well as our myths and legends. Their beauty has inspired our poets and artists. This book celebrates trees from around the world in all their majestic beauty, astonishing diversity, and versatility.

THE TREE:
WONDER OF THE NATURAL WORLD

WHAT IS A TREE?

The first tree evolved over 370 million years ago in the form of Archeopteris, complete with a woody trunk, branches that attached themselves to the trunk in the same way as modern trees, and a root system. The arrival of Archeopteris as a widespread plant form played a critical part in the Earth's developing ecosystem, filtering out the high levels of carbon dioxide present in the atmosphere at that time and creating conditions in which new land animals could evolve. Throughout

Left: The gnarled stump of an ancient Oriental Plane tree, which is closely related to the London Plane, a species common in cities due to its ability to tolerate pollution.

the subsequent eras, trees continued to thrive and evolve. Conifers, tree ferns, and Gingko trees appeared during the triassic era (245–208 million years ago); many of today's trees first grew during the tertiary era (65–2 million years ago). Trees continue to be highly successful life forms; in many parts of the world they are the climax plant species, meaning that any untended land will become dominated by trees.

The trunk, a defining characteristic of a tree, forms around 60 percent of the total mass of any tree. A tree's trunk is key to its success as a plant, allowing it vital access to light, which the tree turns into food through a process called photosynthesis. The higher the tree can bring its leaves, the less competition for light there will be. The trunk, together with the branches, is part of a tree's internal transport system. The trunk and branches bring water, collected by the roots, to the leaves. It also moves food, produced by the leaves, to the other parts of the tree, including the roots. Incredibly, the only living cells in a tree's trunk and branches are in the area just beneath the tough, outer, waterproof bark. This fact explains how a tree can have a hollow trunk, as many ancient trees do, and yet continue to survive.

The leaves on a tree's branches are the way in which the tree creates food for living and growing. Leaves contain chorophyll, a green pigment, which absorbs light energy from the sun. This energy is then turned by the leaves into food through photosynthesis, during which the leaves absorb carbon dioxide and emit oxygen. Leaves, of course, vary hugely in shape and size, from the short, narrow needles produced by conifers to the Traveller's Palm's immense, broad, 3m (10ft) long leaves. Trees are often categorized as being either broad- or narrow-leafed. Another popular division based on leaves is the one into deciduous trees, which shed all their leaves in the fall, and evergreen trees, which lose some of their leaves throughout the year. Evergreens have tough leathery leaves that can cope in extreme climate conditions, including drought and bitter cold. Despite their diverse appearance, however, leaves always perform the same function.

A tree's root system makes up around 20 percent of a tree's mass, as do its branches. Roots function, of course, as an anchor for the tree's tall structure, connecting it to the ground. Roots also work for the tree, however, drawing moisture and minerals from the ground. Despite the great heights that trees can grow to, most trees are comparatively shallow-rooted, with their roots found within 60cm (24in) of the surface; this, of course, makes them susceptible to being blown over in a storm. While tree roots don't penetrate very deep into the ground, they do spread out considerably to form a wide radius around the trunk, becoming finer and finer the farther away they are from the trunk and sometimes forming a radius twice as large as the visible crown on top of the tree.

Certain tree species have evolved different types of roots to suit the environment in which they grow. Rainforest trees are especially shallow-rooted, to make the most of the nutrients in the upper surface of the soil before they are washed away, and consequently have buttress roots, which grow around the trunk above the ground and shore up the tree exactly as a buttress on a cathedral would. Certain trees have adapted to growing in waterlogged conditions, with America's Swamp Cypress producing aerial roots known as "knees." Mangrove trees successfully live in salty water by developing prop roots (which grow from their trunks) and drop roots (which grow from their branches). These roots collect the oxygen which is needed to desalinate the water before it is sent through the tree's system. Certain trees, including the Weeping Fig, have developed what are known as pillar roots. These are fast-growing roots that the tree sends down from its branches into the ground, where they root and form pillarlike supports for the tree. One particularly impressive example of a pillar-rooted tree is a famous Banyan tree in Calcutta's Indian Botanical Gardens, thought to be over 240 years old. Covering an area 275m (300 yards) wide, with its canopy 420m (460 yards) wide and supported by 2,800 pillar roots, it resembles a forest rather than a single tree.

Pollination, which is essential for trees to reproduce, is carried out in a number of ways. Insects are the world's prime pollinators, but in the colder, northern regions, where insects are less common, trees rely on wind pollination, with many temperate trees such as Hazels and Birches producing catkins, abundantly coated in loose pollen which can easily blow away. In the tropics, birds, as well as insects, are important pollinators. Many trees, such as the Jacaranda with its delicate mauve flowers or the Frangipani, have strikingly colorful or fragrant flowers in order to attract birds and insects. Less well known is the fact that bats are key pollinators for many trees, including the South American Calabash tree and the African Tulip tree. Trees that rely on bats for pollination characteristically produce large flowers that open at night and have a strong, though not necessarily pleasant, scent. Leaf-eating animals, such as giraffes or lemurs, can also act as pollinators.

Once pollinated, a tree needs to disperse its seeds as widely as possible to insure its species' survival, and trees have consequently developed a number of ways to encourage dispersal. Many trees are prolific seed producers because the chance of the seed successfully growing into a tree is slender.

Below: English Oaks covered in moss and lichen grow in Wistmans Wood, Devon, England.

A Beech tree, however, only produces a full crop of its seeds (known as beech mast) every five years, in what is known as a "mast year." Many trees produce fruits or berries as edible seed containers in order to tempt birds and animals such as squirrels, monkeys, and, indeed, humans to eat them and so disperse them. Trees also produce their seeds in the form of edible nuts, ranging widely in size from pine nuts to coconuts. Tree-living animals, such as squirrels and monkeys, are very important nut dispersers. In the Amazon rainforest, which in many parts is flooded every year, certain trees rely on fish to eat and disperse their seeds. Some species, such as the Sycamore and the Ash, grow their seeds with extended wings, known as keys, to help the seeds travel farther in the air.

Trees are able to grow in many different environments all around the globe, from the harsh, arid environs of deserts to the water-saturated mangroves, defeated only by the thick ice and bitter cold of the Arctic and Antarctic regions.

There are three main types of forest: tropical, boreal, and temperate. Tropical forests grow along the Equator in Africa, Asia, and South America, and in Australia and the Caribbean. In contrast, boreal forests, dominated by conifers, grow in the cold north, where the trees have to undergo long, harsh winters, with temperatures as low as $-94°F$ ($-70°C$). The conifer's characteristic sloping shape enables heavy snow to slide off the tree without damaging the branches in the process. Temperate forests, often rich in broad-leafed trees, are found mainly in the northern hemisphere, in places that have a moderate climate.

In temperate forests, one species can dominate, so, for example, it's possible to talk of oak woods, beech woods or maple woods. In the tropics, however, many species can be present in one forest, hence the umbrella term "rainforest." In a patch of forest the size of a football field, a temperate forest may have ten trees while a similar-sized patch of rainforest might have 200 types of tree. Despite the diversity of species present in a rainforest, many tropical rainforest trees closely resemble each other, typically possessing tall, thin trunks supported by buttress roots, comparatively small crowns, and evergreen leaves. These characteristics reflect the ferocious competition for space and light among trees in a tropical rainforest.

Palm trees, which perhaps to most people are the archetypal tropical tree, are monocotyledonous plants, that is, plants whose seed embryos contain only one "leaf." Tropical trees usually possess pointed tips on their leaves, allowing them to shed excess water during heavy rainstorms. The warm, wet environment in which they grow means that the fastest growing trees in the world are tropical ones.

Left: The vivid colors of the foliage contrast with the soft gray limestone of the landscape.

VENERABLE AND GIANT TREES

Trees are our world's oldest living things, with temperate trees, in particular, capable of living for many centuries. It's a common misapprehension that great size equals great age. For many years the towering Giant Redwoods in California were assumed to be the world's oldest trees. We now know that, although many Redwoods have reached a great age, they are not the oldest trees on earth. In fact, the trees that live for the greatest ages do not reach the heights achieved by other, younger trees.

Trees, whose trunks grow outwards, are customarily dated by the counting of their growth rings. This form of dating involves either chopping down the tree or using a tree borer to extract wood from the trunk. Not every species possesses regular rings, however, and since many ancient trees are, in fact, hollow, counting rings is by no means a way of gaining a complete picture.

California is home to the oldest known living individual trees in the world, a grove of Bristlecone Pines (whose Latin name *Pinus longaeva* hints at their longevity) growing in the White Mountains of California. Dr. Edward Schulman spent over 20 years studying this grove, and in 1957 he discovered that many of them were over 4,000 years old, while one of them, known as Methuselah after the long-lived prophet in the Bible, is considerably older, having reached well over 4,700. Unlike many other ancient trees, the Bristlecones have retained their cores so Schulman was able to remove core samples and count the growth rings. The Bristlecones' longevity is related to the

Below: Red Mangrove roots spread and seek out nutrients from the flooded ground, but their trunks and leaves remain above the waterline. Tap roots which filter out salt enable them to survive in deltas and coastal waters.

harshness of the environment in which they grow. Growing at a high altitude in semi-arid mountain ranges, the Bristlecones are an extremely hardy and slow-growing species. In the most exposed environments the trees cease to grow any higher once they have reached around 9m (30ft), twisting themselves instead into extraordinarily contorted shapes and bearing just a few leafing branches.

In Great Britain, the title of oldest tree is given to Scotland's Fortingall Yew, estimated to be between 3,000 and 5,000 years old, which grows in a churchyard in the village of Fortingall in Perthshire. The tree was measured in 1769 when its girth had reached 16m (52ft); today only a shell of its great trunk remains. Oaks, of course, with their craggy grandeur, are commonly credited with living to a great age, and a number in Europe are thought to be over 1,500. One of England's ancient Oaks is Kett's Oak at Wymondham in Norfolk, under which Robert Kett rallied support for a rebellion against the Crown in 1549. Robert Kett was condemned for treason and hanged the following year, but the great Oak under which he met is still alive.

All around the world ancient trees are living landmarks, commemorating many different events from coronations and spiritual enlightenment to battles and hangings. Trees, of course, also marked ancient boundaries and formed easily identifiable meeting places. One of Japan's oldest Ginkgo trees grows within the grounds of the Buddhist temple at Zempukuji (since in Japan Buddha is thought to have gained

enlightenment under a Ginkgo rather than a Bo tree, as in Indian Buddhism). This huge, impressive tree, with a girth of around 10m (30ft), is thought to have been planted in 1232.

Once Britain was dominated by woodland; today, however, only 2 percent of ancient woodland (that is woodland that has existed since 1600) remains in the United Kingdom. Of the ancient trees that remain, many are vestiges of the Royal Hunting Forests. Long-established woodland is a very important wildlife habitat, typically containing much richer ground flora than more recently established woods. Ancient mixed woodland also harbors a far wider range of mammals, birds, insects, fungi, mosses, and lichens than modern woodland.

A fascinating discovery in the last century was that of a "living fossil," a tree that had only previously been known from its fossilized remains. The Dawn Redwood was discovered in a very remote part of China and it was only when leaf specimens from the tree reached a botanical institute in Peking in 1946 that its significance was realized. This magnificent, tall tree, with its striking orange-pink fall foliage, is today protected in China and has become a popular species for ornamental planting in Europe and North America.

The largest single living thing on earth in terms of volume is also a tree, a Giant Redwood known as General Sherman, in California's Sequoia National Park, which stands 82.6m (271ft) tall and has a diameter of 8.2m (27ft). It's estimated that the tree contains enough wood to make 630,096 board feet of timber. California also boasts the world's tallest tree, a Coastal Redwood known as the Stratosphere Giant which in 2002 measured 112.6m (369ft 4.8in). Great Britain's tallest trees are both Douglas Firs, growing in Scotland, each around 62m (203ft) tall. Sadly, of course, many of the world's oldest and tallest trees have been cut down by man over the centuries.

Above: Sunset at Madre de Dios in the Amazon basin.

USEFUL TREES

One only has to look around a room in one's home to realize what a wide and diverse role trees play in man's life. Our homes are filled with wooden furniture, our books and newspapers are made from pulped trees, while many of our everyday foods, including bananas, apples, and oranges, all come from trees.

Trees have long played an important part in man's mercantile history. Europe's demand for costly, fragrant spices, such as nutmeg, found only in the tropics, was one of the forces that laid the foundations for European colonies. A look at a handful of tree-related products and their history gives a fascinating picture of how important trees are.

China is the historic home of the silk industry, one of the oldest known textile fibers. Silk is made from the cocoons of silkworms and for at least 5,000 years the Chinese have cultivated the White Mulberry tree, upon whose leaves silkworms solely feed. An old Chinese proverb says: "Patience and perseverance turns Mulberry leaves into the silken robes of a queen." Silk, used to clothe Chinese emperors and their courts, became an important commodity, hence the naming of the Silk Road, a key trade route between China and the West, first used around 100 B.C. The secret of silk manufacture was fiercely guarded by the Chinese and the Persians, but by the sixth century knowledge of the process had reached Europe. Over the centuries, various attempts were made to establish a silk industry in England. In 1608 James I decreed that "every Englishman should cultivate a mulberry tree" and free seeds were issued to encourage planting, with four acres planted on the site of what is now Buckingham Palace. This attempt to establish a silk industry in England failed and it's commonly thought that the wrong type of Mulberry tree was planted, that is the Black Mulberry rather than the White Mulberry which is essential to the silkworms' diet.

In the nineteenth century a rather more successful attempt was made by the British to cultivate a tree that they considered useful. Rubber, which humans have used for everything from tires to rubber bands, is made from the thick sap of a number of plants. The Indians of South America are thought to have been the earliest people to understand rubber's properties. European interest in rubber and its waterproof and elastic properties developed in the eighteenth century. The discovery in 1839 that rubber could be stabilized through a process called vulcanization made the material more commercially viable. It was realized that the most successful rubber

Below: The blossom of an Apple tree is designed to attract insects that will pollinate the tree. Trees pollinated by wind have less showy flowers but often produce significantly more pollen.

plant was a variety called Hueva, native to Brazil, where it grew wild in the rainforest, and Brazil experienced a rubber boom. Attempts were made to cultivate rubber, with the view to creating rubber plantations in Britain's southeast Asian colonies. By 1876 a cargo of rubber seeds had arrived safely in London from Brazil, been grown into plants and sent across to southeast Asia. Britain's botanical gardens, primarily at Kew and Singapore, played a major part in successfully cultivating rubber outside Brazil. Initial attempts saw little success, but perseverance was eventually rewarded, with over 1 million rubber seedlings being planted on the Malay Peninsula in 1899. The demand for rubber was fueled by the rise of the motor car industry and the consequent demand for pneumatic rubber tires (which John Boyd Dunlop had developed in 1888), creating a buoyant market. The British, therefore, introduced the rubber tree to a different continent, profoundly damaging Brazil's economy in the process. Once the source of 98 percent of the world's rubber, it now produces only 5 percent. Today, however, rubber plantations cover over a million hectares in southeast Asia.

All around the world, for hundreds of years, different trees have been valued for their medicinal properties. The Ginkgo tree has long played an important part in Chinese herbal medicine, while in India the Neem tree is valued for the medicinal oil produced from its seeds and a tonic extracted from its bark. Willow bark and leaves were traditionally used as a painkiller; today we use aspirin, derived from salicylic acid, found in Willows. One of the most famous medicines derived from trees is quinine, which comes from the bark of the Cinchona tree from Peru. Peruvian Indians had a wide knowledge of the tree's medicinal properties, using it to treat skin diseases and intestinal problems. In 1633 a monk living in Peru described how Cinchona bark could be ground into

a powder and used to treat fever. Slowly, and against much opposition from established European medical opinion, quinine's efficacy against malaria became recognized. The Jesuits, with their extensive South American connections, shrewdly began organizing the harvest and export of the drug to Europe, where it was known as "Jesuits' bark" or "Jesuits' powder." Aristocratic patients who benefited from this newly discovered, bitter-tasting drug included the Countess of Chinchón, the wife of the Spanish Viceroy in Peru, after whom the tree was named. The story goes that England's King Charles II, too, was cured of malaria by a physician using a secret medicine which was, in fact, quinine. As the European powers expanded their colonies into the tropics the demand for quinine grew considerably. As early as the late eighteenth century, fears were expressed that the Cinchona tree was being over-harvested and might become extinct in the wild. These fears, along with the expense of importing quinine from South America, led in 1858 to a Cinchona-hunting expedition to South America being organized jointly by Britain's India Office and the Royal Botanic Gardens at Kew. The expedition was to endure much adventure and hardship, but in December, 1860, one of the party, plant hunter Richard Spruce, successfully sent back over 600 Cinchona seedlings and nearly 100,000 seeds to Kew. The British were consequently able to set up Cinchona plantations in India, while the Dutch successfully grew a higher-yielding variety of Cinchona in Indonesia. Today, quinine trees continue to be grown and their bark carefully harvested in much the same way as 150 years ago. As strains of the malarial parasite have developed resistance to the synthetic antimalarial drugs, interest in natural quinine is reviving.

Trees, of course, are also the sources of many diverse foods and drinks, from chocolate, made from the pods of the Cocoa tree, to nuts, including walnuts, pine nuts, and pecans. The Palm family is a particularly abundant source of food and drink, with coconuts, dates, sago, palm sugar, palm hearts, and palm wine all coming from Palm trees. One tree-derived beverage which is now widely consumed around the world is coffee. The Coffee tree is native to Africa, with Ethiopia traditionally credited as the home of the dark, bitter drink known as coffee. An Ethiopian legend tells of a goatherd named Kaldi in around A.D. 300 who noticed that his goats were particularly frisky when they ate the red berries of a tree. He tried the berries himself and discovered that he too felt especially awake. The beans, of course, were from the Coffee tree and it was discovered that they could be dried and roasted to make a fragrant drink. Coffee's popularity spread through the Middle and Near East and reached Europe. Britain's first coffee house opened in Oxford in 1650, followed two years later by one in London's Cornhill, opened by Pasqua Rosee. This exotic new drink was noted for its stimulating properties, with Rosee claiming that his coffee was "a very good help to digestion, quickens the spirits, and is good against sore eyes, dropsy, gout and the King's evil" (sic). Coffee rapidly became a fashionable drink in Europe and this profitable new market saw coffee plants being planted by the Dutch in Indonesia while the Spanish introduced Coffee trees to the Caribbean, Central America, and Brazil, which today is the world's largest coffee producer.

Previous page: The sinuous buttress roots of a Picabeen Palm.

Left: Sitka Spruce growing in the Sitka National Park, Alaska. White and Sitka Spruces are two of the species whose range extends farthest north in America.

WOOD

Trees are one of our planet's precious renewable natural resources, valued throughout human history for their wood, which could be used for fuel, to build homes, to make furniture, and for many other purposes. Woods from different trees have different qualities lending themselves to diverse purposes, so long-lasting oak timbers were used in churches and cathedrals, while fine-grained hard box wood was prized for wood engravings and used to make small wood-turning products such as chessmen and small pulley blocks. Yew wood, which is heavy but elastic, was traditionally used for longbows and spears, with one of the world's oldest wooden artifacts being a yew spear found in England, around 150,000 years old. One of the lightest known woods is balsa, which weighs just 9kg per cubic meter (7lb per cubic foot); its ability to float makes balsa a popular wood for rafts and floats. Close-grained teak wood, from the Teak tree, is much prized for its beauty and used for furniture. Mahogany, another much-prized wood noted for its durability and resistance to woodworm, comes from a number of tree species native to South and Central America. Ebony, the product of more than one type of tree, is most famous as the timber used to make pianos' black keys.

Although we live in an age of plastic and metal, a number of traditional crafts continue to use wood and to prize its particular qualities. Spruce and maple are the primary woods used in constructing violins, with spruce valued because it is at once light, strong, and flexible. Violin makers prefer to use wood from old trees that have grown at high altitudes on a mountainside. The wood must be cut during the cold months, when the tree is dormant, and must then be seasoned for many years. The city of Venice is home to a handful of gondola workshops, which continue to construct Venice's most famous craft. Traditionally, gondolas were made with oak wood from trees which had been bent as they grew to produce a continuous grain along the curve. Today, however, a number of different woods, ranging from oak and elm to larch and fir, are used in gondola construction. The distinctively shaped *forcola* (the gondola's oarlock), a masterpiece of design, is traditionally made from walnut wood and is carved by a separate school of artisans who specialize only in making *forcole*.

The coppicing of trees dates back to neolithic times, when it was discovered that a mass of straight branches would grow from certain types of trees (including Hazel, Birch, and Ash) if they were regularly cut at or just above ground level. The word "coppice" comes from the French *couper*, which means to cut. This process was not only sustainable, it actually prolonged the life of the trees used in this way. The length of time between cutting varies according to species and the use of the wood, so birch for broom handles could only be cut every ten to fifteen years, while ash for walking sticks could be cut every four to seven years. Historically, cutting was done in late fall and winter, when there was less agricultural work to be done, with the tree responding vigorously to this treatment with new spring growth. Coppicing provided wood for industrial as well as rural use. In the mid-nineteenth century, England's textile industry is estimated to have used 1,500 million bobbins annually, around half of which were made from coppiced Birch and Alder. Young Willow stems have been cut and used for basket-making since ancient times, with the technique known by the Ancient Egyptians. The early nineteenth century saw an expansion of the willow industry in England, due to the Napoleonic blockades which prevented willow imports from Flanders entering England. Willow stems were used for weaving baskets, essential for carrying goods to market, for hurdles and fish traps.

Pollarding, from the word "poll" for head, was another traditional way of managing trees, with branches cropped for wood or foliage 2–5m (6–15ft) above ground, again at regular periods. This enabled trees to be grown successfully and productively in pastures and parks containing grazing animals. Correctly done, pollarding, like coppicing, has a beneficial effect on trees, contributing to their longevity.

Mankind has been cultivating and managing trees for many centuries. The Ancient Egyptians grew plantations of Sandalwood for its incense, while olive groves are among our earliest cultivated trees. The need to be responsible when it came to using trees and their timber was recognized as long ago as 1664, when John Evelyn wrote "Sylvia – a Discourse of Forest Trees and the Propagation of Timber" to protest the

Above: The practice of growing trees in containers, known as bonsai, is thought to have originated in China but was developed into a high art by the Japanese, with the skill lying in producing a miniature tree which yet looks totally natural.

overuse of trees and to promote more tree-planting. Evelyn's plea is, of course, still relevant today. Plantations of fast-growing conifers are now widely planted for the commercial timber trade, with their pulp used for paper-making. Plantation woodlands, which usually consist of just one species, notably a conifer, do not offer the same ecological variety as permanent coppiced woodland. The lack of permanence of a modern plantation, inherent in its very reason for being planted, restricts the diversity of its wildlife. Many plantations are of exotic species and this too inhibits wildlife diversity. Generally speaking, the longer a tree species has been in a country, the more species of invertebrates and fungi will be associated with it, hence the diversity of wildlife associated with Oak trees in the British countryside. There is now an increasing recognition that forestry needs to be more deeply sustainable.

TREES IN MYTH, RELIGION, AND FOLKLORE

Mankind's relationship with trees has long had a spiritual aspect to it. The idea of a sacred grove of trees, in which enlightenment could be sought and spirits propitiated, is found in many cultures around the world including Ancient Greece and the Native Americans. In Buddhism, Buddha attained enlightenment while sitting under a Bo tree; a temple in Anuradhapura in Sri Lanka houses a Bo that is claimed to be the very tree. The Ancient Greeks believed that trees were home to nymphs, known as dryads. One beautiful nymph, called Daphne, was turned into a Bay tree to escape the god Apollo's amorous advances, with a grief-stricken Apollo declaring that henceforth the bay, or laurel, wreath would be used to crown champions. Certain trees were associated by the Ancient Greeks with the gods, with the Oak held to be Zeus's tree, perhaps because of its propensity to be struck by lightning, Zeus's weapon. In English country folklore, certain trees were thought to offer protection, with Holly leaves carried to ward off lightning and Rowan trees planted by houses to keep away the evil spirits. The tradition of dancing round a maypole has its roots in an ancient spring festival, celebrating the earth's fertility, and used to involve fetching a tree from a forest to use as the pole.

In Norse mythology, Yggdrasil, a huge spreading Ash tree, is the pillar of the world, holding together the "nine worlds." The tree, with its hidden but vital root system, is a powerful image of the interconnectedness of life, an idea referred to when we talk of the "family tree" in genealogy.

In Christianity, too, the tree makes many appearances. It is through eating the fruit from the Tree of Knowledge of Good and Evil that Adam and Eve are cast out from Eden while, of course, Christ dies to redeem mankind on a cross made from wood.

Evergreen trees, such as Holly with its blood-red berries, have been valued in Europe since pagan times, offering a symbol of new life and rebirth even in the dark, cold winter months. Many of the customs that became Christmas traditions over the centuries, such as the burning of a Yule log on the hearth or the wassailing of the orchards, in fact date back to pre-Christian winter solstice festivals. Today, of course, households in countries around the globe celebrate Christmas by setting up an evergreen tree (real or plastic) in their home and decorating it.

For centuries trees have been planted purely for ornamental purposes. Many of the trees that grace our parks and backyards, from the Cedar of Lebanon to the Tulip tree, were introduced from faraway countries and different continents. Europe in the seventeenth and eighteenth centuries saw the rise of the professional plant hunter, undertaking long, and often hazardous, expeditions to distant countries specifically to bring back new plant species.

Because of the length of time that trees take to grow, the planting of trees is very much something undertaken for posterity. When one admires a majestic old Oak in the grounds of a stately home or walks down an avenue of tall, shady trees, one can only thank the vision which inspired people to plant trees for future generations, trees that they themselves would never see mature. Today trees are an important element in town-planning, appreciated for their ability to reduce air pollution in car-congested cities and to reduce the risk of flooding. In hot climates, trees, of course, are natural parasols, offering welcome shade. The Romans planted avenues of trees to provide shade for their troops to march under and the idea was taken up by Napoleon. Trees also enhance urban streets visually, with properties on tree-lined streets selling for higher prices than those on streets lacking trees.

TREES IN PERIL

Today, perhaps more than at any other time, we know how essential trees are for life on Earth. Sadly, however, around the world natural forests continue to vanish under the loggers' implacable saws, with an estimated 40 hectares (100 acres) of forest disappearing every minute. Ten percent of the world's species of trees are threatened with extinction. Once these precious and diverse habitats have been lost, they cannot be quickly and easily replaced. Instead of exploiting trees in the short term, mankind needs to look to the future and work to harvest trees and their resources in a sustainable fashion. It's vital that we appreciate this wonderful resource our planet has given us and treat trees with the respect they deserve.

Left: Pines cover a Pacific island off the south coast of New Caledonia, a reminder of how much of the Earth would have looked before the intervention of man.

CONIFERS

Above: The Ginkgo tree is an extraordinary living fossil, the sole survivor of a primitive group of trees which flourished 200 million years ago and of which fossil remains have been found. It is a sacred tree in Japanese Buddhism, planted in temples, while ginkgo nuts are a prized delicacy in both China and Japan. One Ginkgo tree, in particular, holds a special place in Japanese society, a tree now known as the Hiroshima Ginkgo. Just 1.1km (.68m) away from the blast center of the atomic bomb that fell on the city of Hiroshima in 1945, this tree, by the site of a destroyed temple, budded the following spring and became a national symbol of hope. Today, the temple has been rebuilt around the tree in order not to disturb its roots and on its trunk is engraved "No more Hiroshima."

Opposite: The slow-growing Yew grows to a great age, with Britain's oldest tree being the Yew at Fortingall, Scotland. In Britain, the tree is traditionally associated with churchyards, with at least 500 churchyards in England and Wales containing Yew trees, many of them older than the churches themselves.

Left: For centuries, gardeners have deliberately planted trees in parks and gardens for their ornamental value. Here, rows of carefully shaped Yew trees add an impressive formality to the grounds at Hampton Court Palace, near London. Topiary, the art of clipping trees and bushes into decorative shapes, dates back to the Egyptians and Romans, and enjoyed huge popularity in Europe during the fifteenth, sixteenth and seventeenth centuries, with the French Sun King Louis XIV's gardens at the Palace of Versailles a famous example of topiary.

Above: An impressively gnarled Juniper tree marks an oasis in the Ethiopian borderlands.

Right: A solitary Juniper tree in the mountains. A slow-growing tree, Juniper is valued for its hard, fine-grained wood, with its fragrant scent of incense. The aromatic blue berries are used in cooking, but most famously are an essential ingredient of gin.

Right: The imposing trunks of the Giant Redwood or Wellingtonia tree, native to North America but named in honor of Britain's General Wellington. Giant Redwoods are among the largest of all trees on our planet. While the Redwood tree was held to be sacred by the Native Americans, California's Redwood groves were intensively logged in the nineteenth century.

John Muir, the founder of California's Yosemite National Park, wrote of the Redwoods: "So harmonious and finely balanced are even the mightiest of these monarchs in all their proportions that there is never anything overgrown or monstrous about them."

Previous pages: Swamp Cypress trees in Florida. As the name suggests, the Swamp Cypress can cope with waterlogged conditions, producing aerial roots known as "knees" which grow out of the water or wet ground to gain access to the air. In the fall, their needle-like foliage changes color to spectacular effect.

Left: A Coastal Redwood forest. Slender Coastal Redwoods or Sequoia, like Giant Redwoods, achieve an enormous height and are the tallest trees in the world. Their tall, slightly tapering trunks remain free of branches for up to 45m (150ft), almost the same height as the Statue of Liberty. Today they are found only in a narrow strip of land on the Californian and Oregon coasts. With forest fires a very real threat, it is fortunate that these trees can regenerate from their stumps.

Above: A sprig of Coastal Redwood cones, with the cones measuring only 2–3cm ($^{3}/_{4}$ –1$^{1}/_{4}$ in) long.

Left: This towering tree, reaching up majestically into the clouds, is a Giant Redwood in California's King's Canyon National Park known as General Grant. The title "largest tree in the world" is a disputed one, but with a circumference of over 32.6m (107ft) and at a height of over 81.7m (268ft), there is no doubt that the General Grant is one of the largest trees, and, therefore, one of the largest living things, in the world. Its age is estimated to be between 1,800 and 2,700 years.

Above: The Lawson Cyprus, native to North America, is a popular tree in many parts of the world, widely planted in parks, gardens and hedges. It's noted for its diversity of cultivars, which vary considerably in foliage, color, and form.

Above: Two Douglas Fir trees tower impressively in the snowy Scottish Highlands. Named after the Scottish plant hunter David Douglas who introduced it from America to Britain, this conifer is Britain's tallest tree, with the honors going to two specimens in Scotland each measuring 62m (203ft) tall. The Douglas Fir is an important timber tree, planted commercially in Europe, North America, Australia, and New Zealand and used widely in construction work.

Right: An ancient Greek Fir tree on the slopes of Mount Enos in Cephalonia. This large tree thrives on rocky limestone slopes and can grow at elevations as high as 1,000m (3,280ft).

Above: Snow-covered Norway Spruce cones are a deliciously wintry sight. The Norway Spruce is known as Europe's Christmas tree, and consequently is today cultivated on a large scale. Evergeen trees have played a part in North European religious festivals since pagan times, valued for offering an image of fertility in the dark, cold winter months. It was during Victorian times that the custom of having a Christmas tree in one's home gained wide popularity, thanks to Queen Victoria and her consort Prince Albert, who brought over the tradition from his native Germany.

Right: Shafts of light coming down through the trees in a coniferous forest make a striking sight.

Left: A shapely Pine stands in splendor against a scenic backdrop of China's Yellow Mountains. For centuries Chinese and Japanese artists have delighted in depicting Pine trees with their distinctive foliage.

Above: A Bristlecone Pine in the White Mountains, California. A Bristlecone Pine from these mountains, nicknamed "Old Methuselah," has been dated by scientists at over 4,000 years, making it the oldest living tree yet discovered.

Previous pages: This dramatically twisted, weatherbeaten Jeffrey Pine standing guard on Sentinel Dome in the majestic landscape of California's Yosemite National Park demonstrates how trees grow even in the harshest environments.

Left: A characteristically gnarled and twisted Bristlecone Pine in the White Mountains, California, and a Bristlecone Pine cone (above). This extremely hardy, slow-growing tree survives in the harsh conditions of these mountains, growing at an altitude of 2,400–3,000m (8–10,000ft) in a climate where the average temperature is merely 50°F (10°C) and annual rainfall only 30cm (12in). Once the trees reach between 4.5 and 9m (15 and 30ft) they cease to grow any taller, forming instead into these convoluted and tortuous shapes.

Right: A pine forest in northeastern Greece. In both Greece and Turkey, pine forests are used to house beehives during the summer months, resulting in a dark, aromatic honey much prized in both countries. In Greece, too, pine resin is used to flavor retsina wine, giving it a pronounced pine taste.

Opposite: The Scots Pine, the dominant tree in Scotland's native pine forest, is often found gracing a dramatic, rocky landscape and was historically planted to mark drovers' roads and crossroads. Scots pine timber is the strongest softwood, widely used today for construction purposes. The sap's high resin content made it resistant to water, and this, together with its long, straight trunk, meant that historically it was often used for masts and spars.

Above: Golden male flowers of the Scots Pine shed pollen in the spring and then wither.

Right: A monumental Corsican Pine growing at 1,500m (4,923ft) in the Mouflon Reserve on its native island of Corsica. Introduced to Britain in 1759, the Corsican Pine can be distinguished from the Scots Pine by both the length of its needles and their distinctive twist.

Above: Pines in a plantation reach toward the light. Coniferous timber is referred to as "softwood" although some softwoods are harder than broadleaf timbers. Pines, Douglas Fir and Cedar are all durable while Alder, Birch and Poplar are broadleaf species that produce relatively soft wood.

Right: The Kauri Pine has the distinction of being the most tropical genus of the world's conifers, found in the rainforests of southeast Asia and the subtropical forests of Australia and New Zealand. Two giant Kauri trees, the largest living things on New Zealand, were revered by the Maoris who named them the Father of the Forest and the Lord of the Forest and these imposing, majestic trees have somehow survived 200 years of logging which saw many of their fellow giants felled.

Above: The deciduous Japanese Larch, which originates from the mountains of central Honshu, is one of Japan's most important timber trees, planted extensively throughout the country. Its needle-like leaves are a bright green in the spring, dulling to a gray-green in summer, then turning orange in the fall, and it is often cultivated as a bonsai tree in Japanese temple gardens.

Right: The needles on conifer trees such as this Cedar, Pines, Firs, Spruces, Larches, Redwoods, and Yews are very simple, compact leaves. These needles produce food as efficiently for the tree as large leaves, while losing far less water, and so enabling these trees to survive even in conditions where water is scarce.

Above: This majestic Cedar of Lebanon, with its distinctive shape, is the most famous member of the Cedar family, grown for spectacular effect in the gardens of stately homes or parks. Its natural habitat stretches from Mount Lebanon, through the Syrian mountains into the Turkish Taurus Mountains, where it grows abundantly. Cedar wood has biblical associations; it is thought to be the tree from which King Solomon had his temple in Jerusalem built. Its scented, pink-colored wood was highly prized for cabinet work and interior decoration.

Right: Lichen-covered trunks of two Incense Cedar trees stretch up into the skies. The Incense Cedar is a native of western North America and its aromatic, soft, light brown timber was traditionally used for shingles, sleepers, doors and window-frames and for cedarwood chests.

BROADLEAF TREES

Left: Willows in winter. There are over 300 species of willow and it is used for a number of purposes. Cricket bats come from the straight-growing Cricket Bat Willow, while the vigorous Osier Willow is essential to the basket-making industry. In around 400 BC Hippocrates recommended an infusion of Willow leaves to relieve pain; today if we have a headache we take aspirin, whose active ingredient is a synthetic equivalent of salicin, which occurs naturally in Willow trees.

Above: The characteristic soft, "furry" flowers of the Willow tree, known as pussy willow, are a traditional sign of spring.

Previous pages: Graceful Weeping Willows, often found by rivers or ponds, are a much-admired tree in China, Europe, and Japan. The tree originated in China, famously featuring on Chinese Willow Pattern plates, and is thought to have been introduced to Europe via the Silk Road.

Left: Rows of cultivated Poplars in Spain offer a lesson in perspective. Poplars' light wood is of little value to the timber trade but its natural buoyancy makes it a popular wood for oars. The Lombardy Poplar, with its distinctive tapering outline, is probably the best-known of the Poplar family, widely planted for its ornamental qualities. Poplar trees were a great source of inspiration to the Impressionist artists in France, notably Monet, who painted many pictures of them.

Previous pages: A row of Poplar trees in Alsace hosts an abundant amount of mistletoe, one of many epiphytes (that is, a plant that grows on another plant) which make their homes in trees.

Left: A pollarded Hornbeam in England, where Hornbeam trees have generally been coppiced. Hornbeam wood is extremely hard and heavy. The tree's name derives from the fact that the wood was traditionally used for yokes, so forming a beam between the cattle's horns. Because of its resistance to wear and tear, the wood is widely used in a number of ways, including in pianos, for pulleys, and for butchers' chopping blocks.

Above: The graceful curved trunks of these Birches on the slopes of the Himalayas are caused by the trees having to accommodate a great weight of snow each winter.

Overleaf: Silver Birches, with their distinctive silvery-white trunks, are a characteristic element of the Russian forest. Despite their dainty appearance, Silver Birches are formidably tough trees able to withstand periods of both drought and extreme cold.

Above: Moss and lichen coat a Silver Birch tree trunk in the New Forest, England. Despite this tree's ancient appearance, the Birch tree is a fast-growing but not a long-lived tree, rarely surviving beyond 100 years.

Left: A Silver Birch against a blue sky makes a striking sight. The Birch tree has been used by humans in a variety of ways, with its water-resistant bark used for canoes by the Native Americans and its twigs for besoms or traditional broomsticks while, in Eastern Europe, birch sap is a major source of sugar.

Left: A grove of Aspen trees put on a spectacular display of fall color in the Rocky Mountains. Deciduous trees shed their leaves in the fall in order to conserve energy during the coming winter months. In many countries, including America and Japan, the foliage of deciduous forests, with their distinctive yellows, reds, and oranges, is a much appreciated sight.

Previous pages: A line of Alders looms out of a flooded meadow in the early morning mist. The Common Alder is noted for its ability to thrive in wet conditions, and alder wood forms the foundations of many of Venice's buildings.

Above: A twig of Aspen displays its vivid fall colors. Aspen leaves, because of the way they hang off their stems, tremble even in the slightest breeze; hence its Latin name, *Populus tremula*. In Welsh folklore it was called the tree that never rests, cursed, so popular belief went, because Christ was crucified on a cross made from aspen wood.

Right: Sunlight shines through the branches of a Japanese Maple tree, a widely cultivated tree, much admired for its elegant-shaped leaves and fall color.

A truly splendid Tupelo tree (opposite) and Maple leaves (above) offer vivid fall color. Deciduous trees in temperate parts of the world are important markers of the changing seasons. They come into blossom and leaf in the spring, bear fruit in the summer, change the color of their foliage in the fall, shed their leaves in the winter then, with the coming of spring, begin the whole cycle once more.

Right: The Maple tree has a special association with Canada, with its distinctive palmeate leaf featuring on the Canadian flag. The sweet sap of the Sugar Maple is famously used to produce maple syrup in both Canada and North America. The sap is tapped during the sugaring period of late March to early April, when the sap is rising, and then boiled and considerably reduced to produce maple syrup. An astonishing 40 gallons of sap are needed to produce only one gallon of syrup, explaining the high cost of true maple syrup.

Left: A Red Horse Chestnut with its characteristic "candles" of dark pink flowers is a wonderful sight in late spring. Native to Greece and northern Albania, the Common Horse Chestnut now grows widely throughout Europe where it is valued for its ornamental qualities. Often over 30m (100ft) tall, it is one of the largest flowering trees in the temperate world. Its unusual name is thought to have derived from the fact that its nuts were apparently used to treat sick horses. Confusingly, it is, in fact, not related to the Sweet Chestnut tree.

Above: Glossy horse chestnuts in their shells are known as "conkers" in Britain and for centuries have been used by children to play a game in which the nuts are threaded onto strings then swung against each other until one conker shatters, a tradition that continues to this day.

Above: Horse Chestnut trees are easily identified by their distinctive, large, palmeate leaves, which unfold in spring from shiny, brown "sticky buds."

Right: For centuries the Sweet Chestnut tree has been valued for its edible, dark brown-shelled chestnuts, with the Greeks introducing them to Europe from their native western Asia and the Romans cultivating them. Culinary uses of the chestnut vary considerably, from cakes and puddings to pasta and soups. In France, chestnuts (*marrons*) are famously turned into *marrons glacés*, a time-consuming process in which the chestnuts are carefully candied by being repeatedly steeped in a sugar syrup. In Britain, chestnuts are traditionally combined with sausagemeat to make stuffing for the Christmas turkey.

Above: The Beech tree's triangular nuts, encased in a prickly shell, are known as "beech mast." Although beech mast can be eaten by humans it was traditionally mainly used as a food for animals, particularly pigs.

Opposite: The graceful Beech tree, with its distinctive smooth, silvery-gray bark, is a much-loved European tree, able to thrive even in shallow chalky soil. Despite the fact that it is one of Britain's tallest broad-leafed trees, reaching up to 40m (130ft), Beech trees are notoriously shallow-rooted and, therefore, sadly susceptible to strong winds, rarely living for more than 200 years.

Overleaf: A beech wood in fall is both a lovely sight and an excellent place to hunt for wild mushrooms.

The Copper Beech, with its distinctive, dark wine-red foliage, is one of nature's quirks. The green chlorophyll of the leaves is hidden by a pigment which colors the leaves a purple-red. Because of their striking color, Copper Beeches are frequently planted for ornamental purposes.

As well as being admired for their beauty, Beech trees were also traditionally valued for their tough, strong timber, widely used in furniture, for flooring, and to make plane blocks. Because the branches retain their dead leaves in winter, Beeches are also popular for hedging.

The name beech derives from the Anglo-Saxon *boc* and the German *buche*, from which the English word book comes. It's thought that early manuscripts and runes were written on thin tablets of beech wood, hence its book-related name and its traditional associations with knowledge and learning.

Above: Oak leaves, with their distinctive shape. In England, sprigs of Oak leaves were traditionally worn on Royal Oak Day (May 29) to commemorate King Charles II's escape from the Roundheads during the Civil War by hiding in an Oak tree.

Right: A magnificent English or Common Oak towers in solitary splendor. The English Oak, as its very name suggests, has long been closely associated with Britain. Widespread across Europe, the English Oak today is the most commonly found tree in British broad-leafed woodlands. Oak wood is one of the finest hardwoods, noted for its strength and durability; the eighteenth-century diarist John Evelyn wrote admiringly of it that "houses and ships, Cities and Navies are built with it." For centuries the Royal Navy was made up of ships built from sturdy English oak. Its timber was not the only useful element of the Oak tree; for centuries the bark of the Common Oak was widely used in the tanning industry.

Previous pages: Ancient Oaks, with their thick, gnarled trunks, are a majestic woodland sight. The English Oak is capable of living for hundreds of years, with the really ancient Oaks invariably hollow and a number of them reckoned to be over 1,000 years old. The Oak has always been widely revered, figuring in Greek and Norse mythology and the Bible, while the Druids too believed it was a sacred tree.

Left: A grove of Cork Oaks, with their surprising "bare" trunks, are a characteristic sight in Spain and Portugal. Cork Oaks can survive having their outer bark stripped off, with the process taking place at nine- to twelve-year intervals. The stripped bark is dried, boiled, then cut to shape, with the resulting cork most famously used for wine bottles, though today the wine industry's move to plastic stoppers or screw-tops is threatening this traditional usage. Oak's other association with the wine industry is the use of oak barrels in which to mature wines, adding a distinctive flavor to the wine in the process.

Previous page: Oak trees in winter. Of all the British trees, the Oak supports the widest variety of insect and other invertebrate life, making it an important mainstay of British forests.

Left: There are almost 600 species of Oak around the world, among them the White Oak which grows in North America. The White Oak is America's most important timber tree, traditionally called the "stave oak" because its hard, durable timber was used to make the staves of barrels.

Above: The Ash tree has long been a favorite with children because of its winged seeds, known as "spinners," which spin through the air as they fall. The Ash has many magical associations, featuring in Norse mythology as the "world tree" holding the universe together and thought to possess healing properties. Its strong, flexible wood was highly prized and used to make spears, walking sticks, wheels and, in more recent times, the wings of the de Havilland Mosquito aircraft.

Above: A cluster of Elm seeds, with each seed carried in the center of a papery disk.

Opposite: A pastoral scene of Elm trees in a meadow. Elm trees were grown for both ornamental and practical reasons, providing timber and also food for cattle. Because of its ability to withstand wet conditions, elm wood was used for water pipes and boat building, while elm piles were laid under bridges and buildings. For centuries tall English Elm trees were a characteristic sight of the English landscape, often filled with noisy, chattering colonies of rooks. In the 1970s, however, Dutch Elm disease had a decimating effect on Britain's mature Elm trees, substantially altering the British treescape.

Overleaf: A line of Elm trees along the edge of a snowy field.

Left: Campbell's Magnolia is a truly magnificent member of the Magnolia family, capable of growing up to 45m (150ft) tall and bearing large, pink, cup-shaped flowers in the spring. Originally from the Himalayan forests, like so many ornamental trees it was deliberately introduced.

Above: The lilac is widely grown in gardens as a small tree or shrub, valued for its pretty white, mauve, or pink flowers and their distinctive heady, fragrant scent.

Overleaf: The beautiful, springtime sight of a Cherry tree orchard in bloom has inspired generations of artists to try to capture the blossom's fragile beauty. In Japan, cherry blossom is greatly prized with a number of ornamental Cherry varieties widely planted in parks and gardens.

Above: An Orange tree, bearing at once its famous fruit and its fragrant white blossom. Originally from southeast Asia, citrus fruits, including grapefruits, lemons, and limes, are today widely grown around the world, with oranges the most popular of all. While sweet oranges are enjoyed for their flesh and juice, bitter oranges, most famously the Seville, are used to make marmalade. Bergamot oil, extracted from the peel of the fragrant bergamot orange, is used widely both in perfumery and to flavor Earl Grey tea.

Today, citrus fruits are valued for their high Vitamin C content. The healthy benefits of citrus juice were recognized by the Royal Navy in 1795 when, in what was to be an effective attempt to beat scurvy, it became compulsory for navy sailors to drink a daily ration of lime juice, hence the American term "limeys" for the English.

Above: The apple is one of the first fruits to have been cultivated and holds a special place in our affections and, indeed, in Western culture. In Greek mythology a golden apple is awarded to Aphrodite by Paris, who chooses her above the other goddesses and thus sows the seeds of the Trojan War. In Christianity, the fruit of the tree of knowledge of good and evil is traditionally depicted as an apple. In Britain, Apple tree wassailing, a tree-blessing ceremony, is thought to date back to the Druids, and is a custom continued by farmers and country folk for centuries to ensure good crops.

The process of grafting Apples to produce better fruit is described as long ago as the second century BC by Cato the Elder. Over the centuries, numerous apple varieties were created through grafting. Apples arrived in America with emigrants to the New World, who brought with them apple pips which would survive the long sea voyage. America's most famous apple grower is Johnny Appleseed, born in Massachusetts in 1775 as Johnny Chapman, who traveled the length and breadth of the country planting Apple seeds.

Left: Delicate Almond blossom appears on the tree in early spring before the tree comes into leaf. Originally from west Asia and cultivated by the Ancient Greeks, the Almond tree is now widely cultivated around the world, with America the main producer. Both bitter and sweet almonds are grown commercially, the former high in poisonous prussic acid which, however, disappears with the application of heat. Sweet almonds are eaten as they are or used in cooking, perhaps most famously in marzipan.

Overleaf: Low-growing Olive trees, with their gnarled, twisted trunks and silver-gray leaves, are an evocative sight of the Mediterranean. In Greek mythology the Olive tree is given by Athene, the Goddess of Wisdom, to the Athenians and the tree has been cultivated in the Mediterranean region since prehistoric times. The Olive tree has long aroused veneration. In the Bible, the dove sent by Noah from the Ark returns with an Olive branch, which has become a symbol of peace. Olive trees are noted for their longevity, thought to be able to survive for 1,500 years, thus making them among Europe's oldest trees.

The Olive was grown primarily for the edible oil which could be extracted from its fruit, with the oil used in cooking, for lighting, and also for anointing the body in religious ceremonies. For hundreds of years, the process of picking the olives by hand and pressing them in stone mills to extract the oil continued in the same way. Olives, themselves, are inedible raw and must be cured before they can be eaten.

Above: Glossy, black elderberries, though inedible raw, were a popular hedgerow harvest, used to make jellies, cordial, and wine.

Right: An Elder tree profusely covered with white elderflowers. In Britain the fragrant blossoms of the Common Elder were traditionally used to make elderflower cordial, with today seeing the cordial enjoying a new popularity and consequently being manufactured on a commercial scale. Elderflower fritters have been enjoyed since medieval times. In North America the Native Americans valued the elderflower for its medicinal properties, using infusions to ward off colds.

Left: A lone Hawthorn tree, bent by the winds, looks out over the rolling Dartmoor landscape.

The slow-growing Hawthorn, which seldom reaches 8m (30ft), with its formidable thorns and spectacular May-time blossom (known as may) has many associations with folklore and religion. Since pagan times, it has been a symbol of fertility and its blossoms were tradionally worn by the May Queen and King in May Day celebrations. In Christian folklore the crown of thorns is said to have been made from hawthorn, though, in fact, the tree does not naturally grow in Palestine. Most famous of the tales around the Hawthorn is the legend of the Glastonbury Thorn. This dates back to the sixteenth century and tells of how Joseph of Arimathea came to Glastonbury in England, where he rested on his staff. During the night the staff rooted into the ground and became a flowering Hawthorn tree, seen as a sign to Joseph that he should found a Christian chapel at Glastonbury. To this very day, a Hawthorn, said to be descended from the original Glastonbury Thorn, grows in the grounds of Glastonbury Abbey and a sprig of this is sent every Christmas to the reigning British monarch.

Right: The Rowan or Mountain Ash is an attractive tree, with its white blossoms in the spring, then orange or scarlet foliage in the fall, followed by clusters of orange berries (pictured above). The Rowan is a tree with many mythic associations, believed in Nordic mythology to have saved the great god Thor from drowning. Rowan trees were often planted near houses to ward off evil spirits, while travelers on Midsummer's Night were advised to carry a sprig of rowan for protection from the fairies active on that night. Tough, strong rowan wood was used for walking sticks, spinning wheels, poles, and whips.

Left: An avenue of Lime or Linden trees is a common sight in European and North American towns and cities, as the tree can thrive despite severe pruning or annual lopping. The name lime, first used in the early seventeenth century, is derived from the older name lind or linden. Lime trees can live to a great age, reaching well over 1,000 years. Pale, soft lime wood is particularly used for piano keys, matches, and carving.

Above: Fragrant Lime or Linden blossom is a popular source of nectar for bees, resulting in a delicious honey.

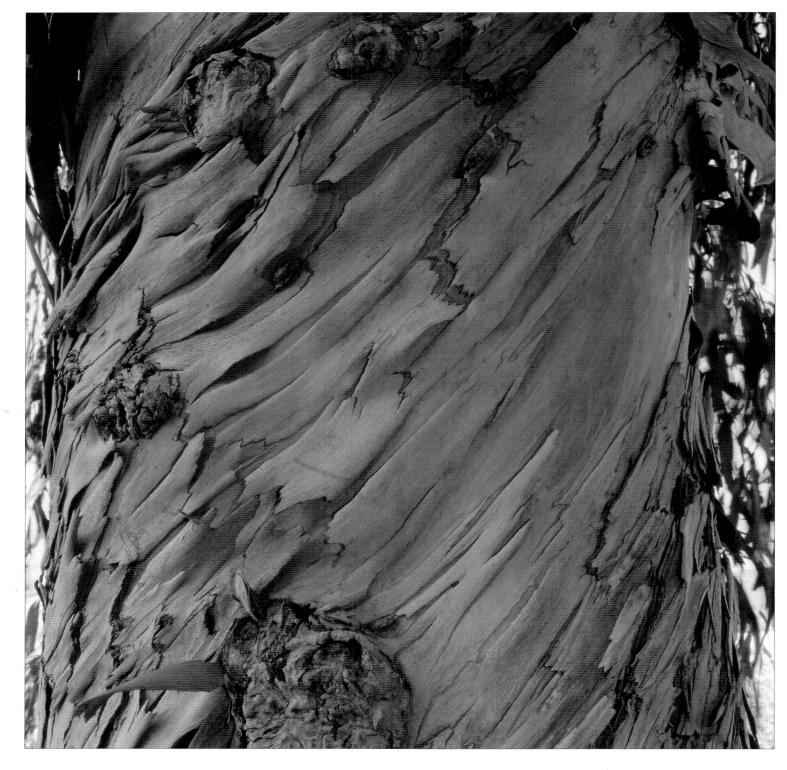

Above: The characteristic peeling bark of a Eucalyptus tree.

Previous pages: Found primarily in Australia, the Eucalyptus or "gum tree" is emblematic of that country. The tree's ability to regenerate itself after forest fire is one reason for its great success on this continent, with many Eucalyptus species able to produce new shoots from resting buds in their bark. Eucalyptus oil, distilled from its leaves, has natural antiseptic qualities and is widely used in medicines and cleaning agents. In order to protect the Eucalyptus from leaf-eating animals, the leaves are poisonous to many animals, as well as being extremely fibrous and low in nutrition. The koala is one of only three mammals that can survive on a diet of Eucalyptus leaves, possessing a slow metabolism that allows it to gradually digest these tough leaves.

Right: The graceful Snow Gum tree is a member of the Eucalyptus family, which boasts over 400 species. Because of their ornamental qualities, the Eucalyptus is now widely grown around the world.

Right: Certain trees are able to thrive in swampy conditions, among them the Paperbark, named for its thick, peeling bark. The Paperbark was deliberately introduced to the Florida Everglades to help reclaim the marshy land, where, however, it has proved too successful. Attempts are now being made to halt its progress, which is altering the Everglades' distinctive habitat.

Above: A forest of Pandan, Figs and Palm trees grows on the banks of the lime-rich waters of Lawn Hill Creek in Queensland, Australia.

Overleaf: The Paperbark forest in swampland is an important Australian habitat, offering a home to many different creatures, including birds, bats, and insects. Remarkably, certain Paperbarks are able to thrive in areas that are flooded for up to eight months a year. The Aboriginals had many uses for the Paperbark tree, using its bark to make huts, in funeral ceremonies, and as a food wrapper.

TREES OF
TROPICAL & ARID REGIONS

Above: Long strands of lichen form an eye-catching sight in a Venezuelan forest. Trees are a favorite home for mosses and lichens.

Left: There are three main types of rainforest: tropical, which grow near the Equator; cloud forests, which grow on mountainsides among the clouds; and temperate rainforests, which grow farther from the Equator in a cooler climate that possesses distinct seasons, in countries including Australia, New Zealand, and North America. Many of the trees in temperate rainforests are conifers, often picturesquely covered in mosses and lichens.

Previous pages: The extraordinary sight of trees growing out of water is a normal one in the world's mangrove swamps. Mangrove trees adapt to their flooded environment by growing "stilt roots," eye-catching raised roots that allow the roots essential access to oxygen. These characteristic stilt roots give the tree the appearance of a large, many-legged creature scuttling through the swamp.

Right: Moss grows abundantly on a Myrtle tree forest in Tasmania. This rare Australasian Myrtle, which today only grows naturally in southeastern Australia, belongs to the group of trees known as Southern or False Beeches, of which the majority are found in South America. This shared biological heritage, plus fossil evidence showing Southern Beeches to have been growing in Antartica around 100 million years ago, demonstrates that the trees were growing during the existence of Gondwanaland the supercontinent, when Australasia, South America, and Antarctica were all joined together, before being separated by tectonic plate movement.

Overleaf: Tropical trees loom up out of the morning mist in Malaysian Borneo.

Right: These spectacularly sinuous buttress roots are a characteristic rainforest sight. In the highly crowded and competitive environs of a rainforest, trees typically have tall, straight trunks, reaching up high toward the light, and root systems that, while spread over a large area, are typically shallow. Buttress roots, which grow from the trunk of the tree, are essential for providing extra stability, exactly in the way that buttresses work supporting cathedrals or fortresses.

Above: The formidable spikes of the Jauary Palm form a daunting natural barrier, protecting the tree from unwelcome attentions. Fascinatingly, the seeds of this Amazon rainforest tree (left) are dispersed by fish, which consume the palm nuts when the forest floods, a prime example of how trees can thrive in diverse environments.

Left: Moroccan Date Palms by the light of the moon form a quintessential oasis image. In North Africa and the Middle East, the fruit of the Date Palm is an important food, with hard dates traditionally a staple of the nomads. Date Palms can reach over 30m (100ft) in height but commercially grown trees are usually felled at 15m (50ft) because of the difficulty of reaching the dates, which are only produced at the top of the palm.

Above: New Zealand's only Palm tree, here with its distinctive strings of fruit dangling down, grows more abundantly on the country's North Island.

Overleaf: Dates grow in large bunches, each weighing over 10kg (20lb) and containing around 1,000 dates.

Above and right: Palm trees, with their striking leaf formations, have long been valued for their ornamental qualities, gracing temples, palaces, and parks in the tropics and imported to furnish conservatories in cooler climes. Human beings, however, have appreciated Palms for more than their decorative appearance. Palms are a valuable source of food (including coconuts, sago, and palm sugar), timber, and thatching, with Palm leaves traditionally used to thatch homes in the tropics.

Overleaf: Palm trees silhouetted against the sky on a tropical beach form a classic fantasy image.

Right: The huge fruits of the Coco-de-Mer Palm are an impressive sight. In fact the coco-de-mer is the largest single-seeded fruit in the world, weighing up to 20kg (44lb) and taking many years to ripen fully. Native only to certain of the isolated Seychelles Islands, the coco-de-mer fruit was for centuries an object of mystery. Occasionally, the huge fruits would float their way across the Indian Ocean and wash up on the shores of south India, the Maldives, Zanzibar, and Sri Lanka, but for a long time their origins remained unknown, hence their name which means coconut of the sea. The nut's distinctive two-lobed shape and rarity led to legends growing up around it, among them that it grew under the sea and had aphrodisiac properties. Coco-de-mer shells were used as bowls and thought to protect against poison. Its source was discovered in 1743. During the 1970s the coco-de-mer fruit became a popular tourist item and today, sadly, the Coco-de-Mer Palm is an endangered species because of over-exploitation.

Left: An avenue of tall, graceful Mango trees offers shade along a rural road in Malaysia. Mangoes are probably the best-known tropical fruit, cultivated in India since at least 2000 BC and now grown widely around the world. For centuries, the cultivation of Mango orchards in India was reserved for rajahs and nabobs. The Portuguese took the Mango from their south Indian colonies to Africa, from where it made its way to Brazil and the West Indies. There are many Mango varieties, with the Alphonso from India particularly well-regarded.

Above: A Strangler Fig, as its name suggests, engulfs its host tree with ruthless efficiency. The Strangler Fig begins life as an epiphyte high in a host tree's branches, growing from a seed deposited by a bird or monkey. First it produces aerial roots, which make their way to the ground and root there until eventually the host tree is suffocated and dies, leaving a Strangler Fig tree with a hollow center.

Above: The curiously shaped seed pods of the Ear Pod tree explain its unusual name. Found in Mexico and Central America, the Ear Pod's seed pods can be eaten when young and are also used as animal fodder. Its wide-spreading canopy means it is widely planted for the shade it offers. An adult tree produces an average 2,000 pods a year, with each pod containing ten to sixteen seeds.

Right: Large breadfruit, with their tough, spiky skins, are a starchy fruit, eaten as a staple in many parts of the tropics. Native to the Pacific islands, the fruit was introduced by the British to their colonies in the West Indies to provide a food source for the slaves on the plantations. Famously, of course, one of those British officers entrusted with bringing breadfruit to the Caribbean was Captain William Bligh on HMS *Bounty* who, while sailing from Tahiti with a cargo of Breadfruit saplings in 1788, was mutinied against and set adrift in a launch. Undaunted, Bligh successfully delivered a cargo of Breadfruit plants to Jamaica in 1793.

Right: Despite its rather undistinguished appearance the Ylang-ylang tree, a member of the Custard Apple family which grows in southeast Asia, India, and the Pacific Islands, is highly prized for its fragrant flowers from which is distilled ylang-ylang oil, widely used within the perfumery industry. The Ylang-ylang tree's scent is particularly strong at night, used to lure the moths which are essential to fertilizing the tree. Flowers (above) are first harvested when the tree reaches five years, with the flowers picked early in the morning. Around 100kg (220lb) of ylang-ylang flowers are needed to produce 1.5–2.5 liters (2$\frac{1}{2}$–4$\frac{1}{2}$ pints) of oil, with the first distillation particularly prized.

Left: The impressive sight of an Australian Spur Mahogany tree reaching for the sky. The Australian rainforest is home to many fascinating trees that are unique to this continent. One of the tree world's most exciting finds in recent years was the discovery in 1994 in a deep rainforest gorge among the Australian Blue Mountains of the Wollemi Pine, a living link to Australia's prehistoric past thought to have died out millions of years ago; the botanical equivalent of finding a live dinosaur today.

Above: The spectacular, cascading yellow flowers of the Indian Laburnum or Golden Shower make this a popular ornamental tree, widely planted in tropical gardens. In Indian Ayurvedic medicine, its bark and roots are used to treat a number of conditions, including fevers, bronchitis, and pneumonia.

Right: One of the most striking trees found in Madagascar and Africa is the Baobab, an awe-inspiring tree which can live for many centuries. Africa's oldest known tree is a Baobab growing in Sagole, South Africa, whose base is nearly 14m (46ft) in diameter, and which is thought to be over 5,000 years old.

Above: The Baobab's large white flowers hang singly from the tree's branches and have a powerful melon-like scent.

Right: The Baobab tree is noted for its huge, swollen, fire-resistant trunk, which it uses to store water during the rainy season. Large, old Baobab trees are thought to be able to hold as much as 1,200 liters (2,100 pints) of water. Its distinctive appearance has given rise to many stories and legends. An Arabic legend recounts how the Baobab was plucked up by the Devil and thrust back upsidedown into the ground, with its roots in the air.

Overleaf: Madagascan Baobab trees are silhoutted imposingly against the backdrop of a colorful sunset.

Above: A Dragon Blood tree offers shady shelter for a woman and her cattle in a parched landscape.

Right: Dragon Blood trees, with their distinctive umbrella-shaped leaf canopies, mark a barren landscape. The evocative name comes from the tree's red resin, known as dragon's blood or cinnabar, which forms on the cherry-sized berries and has been harvested since ancient times. The resin is sold in lumps, beads, sticks, or powder form. Pliny told of how the tree sprang up after a fight between an elephant and a dragon, and dragon's blood was considered a powerful medicine. It was also valued as a pigment and dye, used to stain glass, marble, and Italian violins.

Overleaf: A forest of flat-topped Acacia trees marks the rim of the Ngorongoro crater in Tanzania.

Above: A stinging ants' nest in the swollen thorns of an East African Whistling Thorn tree, an example of an unusual relationship. Rather than nesting in the ground, which is either extremely waterlogged or too hard and dry to tunnel in, the ants choose to make their home in the tree. They tend their home by pruning the tree, nibbling off any axillary growth that might touch other plants, and also actively protect it, rushing out upon the slightest movement to sting any animals, such as giraffes, that might have begun to graze upon the tree

Left: A lone elephant forages for food in an African acacia forest. Elephants can be highly destructive when feeding, often uprooting or pulling down trees in the process and so leaving a trail of devastation.

Overleaf: Dead Camelthorn trees form an eerie "forest" in the arid Namibian desert.

Left: The African Sausage tree's humorous name derives from its large, sausage-shaped seed pods, which can be over 60cm (30 in) long and weigh as much as 6.6kg (15lb). The tree bears strong-smelling red flowers that attract bats, insects, and sunbirds which act as pollinators. The seed pods are not eaten as such but are used in traditional African medicine and were once thought to possess magic powers.

Above: Trees, of course, are vital in providing shelter for birds, as demonstrated by this impressive social weaver's nest.

Overleaf: Quiver trees, a slow-growing member of the Aloe family, are native to Southern Africa and Namibia, where they live in arid areas, developing massive trunks as they grow. The golden-brown bark scales on these trunks are razor-sharp, making the branches of these trees a popular place for weaver birds to nest in as their eggs and young are safe from snakes and jackals.

Left: Despite their modest height and appearance, Frankincense trees have been valued since ancient times for their aromatic white resin, one of the gifts the Magi brought to honor the baby Jesus in Bethlehem. Frankincense is also known as olibanum, with its oil called "Oil of Lebanon." The resin is harvested from the trees twice a year, the trunk of the tree being carefully scraped so that the resin flows from the tree to heal its wound. The resin is aged before selling and varies in color from opaque white to golden-brown, depending on which variety of Frankincense tree it has come from. Valued in Indian Ayurvedic medicine, frankincense is used in cosmetics, soap, and perfumes in the West and as an insecticide in the Middle East. In Ancient Egypt frankincense was used to embalm the dead.

Above: A Tree Aloe grows on a rocky outcrop in the Namibian Desert.

Overleaf: The contorted shape of the Joshua tree is a characteristic sight of the Mojave Desert. The largest of the Yucca family, reaching up to 12m (40 ft) tall, the Joshua tree is said to have been named by the Mormon settlers whom the tree reminded of the Prophet Joshua, with his arms outstretched beckoning them on.

BIBLIOGRAPHY

Burnie, David, *Forest*, (Dorling Kindersley, 1998)

Davidson, Alan, *The Oxford Companion to Food*, (Oxford University Press, 1999)

Dolmaore, Anne, *The Essential Olive Oil Companion,* (Grub Street, 1999)

Ganeri, Anita, *Earth Files Forests*, (Heinemann Library, 2002)

Green, Sephanie and Meyer, Zoe, *Mulberry & Silk*, (Sage Press, 2003)

Greenaway, Theresa, *Jungle*, (Dorling Kindersley, 1994)

Harding, Patrick and Tomblin, Gill, *How to Identify Tree*, (HarperCollins, 1998)

Hora, Bayard (Ed), *The Oxford Encyclopedia of Trees of the World*, (Oxford University Press, 1981)

Johnson, Owen & More, David, *Tree Guide*, (HarperCollins, 2004)

Leathart, Scott, *Whence Our Trees*, (Foulsham, 1991)

Lewington, Richard & Streeter, David, *The Natural History of the Oak Tree*, (Dorling Kindersley, 1993)

Mabey, Richard, *Flora Britannica: the Concise Edition*, (Chatto & Windus, 1998)

Milner, J. Edward, *The Tree Book* (Collins & Brown Ltd, 1992)

Morgan, Sally, *Saving the Rainforests*, (Franklin Watts, 1999)

Musgrave, Toby & Will, *An Empire of Plants*, (Cassell & Co., 2002)

Pakenham, Thomas, *Meetings with Remarkable Trees*, (Phoenix Illustrated, 1997)

Pakenham, Thomas, *Remarkable Trees of the World*, (Weidenfeld & Nicholson, 2002)

Paterson, Jacqueline Memory, *A Tree in Your Pocket*, (Thorsons, 1998)

Russell, Tony & Cutler, Catherine, *The World Encyclopedia of Trees*, (Anness Publishing, 2003)

Trager, James, *The Food Chronology*, (Aurum Press Ltd, 1996)

PICTURE ACKNOWLEDGMENTS

The publisher would like to thank Ardea for kindly providing the photographs for this book.
We would also like to thank the following Ardea photographers for their kind permission to reproduce their pictures:

Ardea 19, 26-27, 37, 38, 51, 56, 58, 59, 71, 86, 90, 91, 96-97, 106-107, 111, 122-123, 131, 134-135, 184-185, 187; Laub 94-95, 124-125;
Pat Morris 179; Chris Martin Bahr 126-127, Liz & Tony Bomford 52, 88; Liz Bomford 166; J B & S Bottomley 115; John Cancalosi 30-31;
Johan De Meester 16, 112-113 (and 4); David Dixon 55, 83, 116-117 151; Steve Downer 81; Thomas Dressler 68-69, 102-103, 150, 180-181;
Jean-Paul Ferrero 20, 44, 87, 133,138-139, 140,142-143, 144-145, 154; Ferrero/Labat 176-177; Kenneth W Fink 29, 36, 114; Paul Germain 84-85;
Bob Gibbons 10, 11, 12-13, 25, 39, 48-49, 50, 70, 75, 76-77, 81, 89, 98 -99, 105, 118 -119, 124 (and 3); Pascal Goetgheluck 40, 57, 62-63, 82, 130;
Francois Gohier 15, 32-33, 45, 46-47 (and 1), 78-79, 141, 162, 188-189; Nick Gordon 148, 149; Chris Harvey 155; Steve Hopkin 60-61; Masahiro Iijima 168-169, 172-173;
Chris Knights 72-73; Jean-Marc La Roque 128-129 (and 190-191); Wayne Lawler 17,132, 146-147;
Tom & Pat Leeson 18; Ake Lindau 6-7, 41, 64, 74, 92-93, 108-109, 120-121; Ken Lucas 152-153; John L. Mason 35, 47, 54, 65, 98, 106, 127,183, 186; Stefan Meyers 156-157,
178; Pat Morris 182; D Parer & E Parer-Cook 161; A P Paterson 24, 110, 120; R F Porter 174, 175; Robyn Stewart 8-9;
Peter Steyn 136- 137, 158-159, 170, 171; J E Swedberg 104 (and 2); Ron & Valerie Taylor 14; Duncan Usher 100-101; Joanne Van Gruisen 1 60, 167; Richard Waller 22-23, 53
(and 193); Adrian Warren 28; M Watson 66-67, 163, 164, 164-165; Wardene Weisser 34, 42-43

Front of jacket picture: Michael Fogden/OSF/Photolibrary.com
Back cover picture: Steve Downer /Ardea
Front flap picture: Wardene Weisser/Ardea
Back flap picture: Ake Lindau/Ardea

This book would not have been possible without the help of Sophie Napier and Su Gooders and all their colleagues at Ardea in London.
Thanks also to Rebecca Marsden, Vicki Harris, Trevor Bunting, Alison Guantlett and Carol Salter.